❧ Siamese Cookery ❧

MARIE M. WILSON

Siamese Cookery

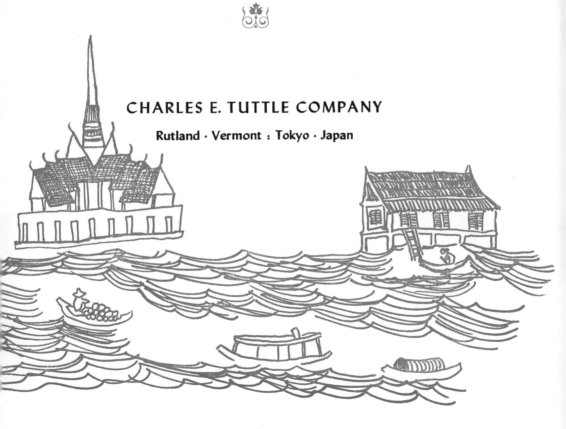

CHARLES E. TUTTLE COMPANY

Rutland · Vermont : Tokyo · Japan

Representatives

Continental Europe: BOXERBOOKS INC., *Zurich*
British Isles: PRENTICE-HALL INTERNATIONAL, INC., *London*
Australasia: PAUL FLESCH & CO., PTY. LTD., *Melbourne*
Canada: HURTIG PUBLISHERS, *Edmonton*

Published by the Charles E. Tuttle Company, Inc.
of Rutland, Vermont & Tokyo, Japan
with editorial offices at
Suido 1-chome, 2–6, Bunkyo-ku, Tokyo

Copyright in Japan, 1965
by Charles E. Tuttle Co., Inc.

Library of Congress Catalog Card No. 65–23329

International Standard Book No. 0-8048-0530-X

First printing, 1965
Fifth printing, 1974

Layout of illustrations by J. Paull
Book design and typography by F. Sakade
PRINTED IN JAPAN

To my husband

*who, for more than a year, tasted
and criticized, and encouraged*

❁ *and* ❁

To my daughter

*who, at the tender age of three,
was also tasting and criticizing*

✿ Table of Contents ✿

🦋 Introduction 🦋

"Just where is Siam?" I asked, as I pored over a map of Asia. The airlines clerk pointed out a pink shape. She handed me the tickets, and, as I gave her the money, my heart sank. In just one week I would be leaving all familiar things behind me and be on my way to a land halfway around the earth to get married. My fiancé, a scholar, was in Bangkok on a grant to teach and to study. With no idea of the country and its climate, its people and their customs, I was both excited and frightened.

At first everything in Bangkok came as a shock. It was so different from home. Here everybody lives outdoors during the day because it is hot and humid. The people's ordinary daily activities—working, bathing, cooking, eating, talking, buying, selling—are in plain view. Most people seemed to have few things according to our standards, but, to my astonishment, they did not seem to mind. The language was strange, and the food even more so. I spent many hours writing home about these differences, but before long they became insignificant. We struggled with the language. We grew to love the food. We tolerated the climate. We even had a baby there. And we came to know the romance of Siam.

It does not take long to realize that the Siamese are a water people. Bangkok, the only large city, and the surrounding countryside are a network of canals that crisscross the Chao Phraya River. Rice boats from up-country, fishing boats, steamboats, and sampans dot the river. Up and down the *klongs* (canals) are store boats containing wonderful wares—coconuts, mangoes, giant squashes, gourds, pumpkins, pots and pans, china, cloth. There are restaurant boats serving curries, coffee, and cakes. And on these boats whole families spend their lives, selling, cooking, and eating, especially cooking and eating which the Siamese love to do. Everywhere, on water or on land, the charcoal stove on which rice is being cooked is fanned by a man, woman, or child. Every hour of the day I saw families squatting in a circle, laughing, talking, and eating their rice. The Thai women wear basket-shaped hats to protect themselves from the tropical sun, and the *pasin*, a skirt made from a wide tubular fabric which is like a sarong, pleated once in front to make it fit and held fast with a belt or just tucked in at the waist. With this they wear a Western-style blouse, having long ago given up the bright scarves which they draped over their bosoms. The men wear khaki pants or shorts, but they bathe in the *pakomah*, a long, wide plaid cloth which a Siamese male can drape modestly into trunks in an amazingly short time.

Plants and trees dominate the Bangkok landscape. Coconut palms overhang the banks of the *klongs,* and, among the lush tropical vegetation, I loved the "flame of the forest," a tree which blazes with crimson blossoms. The houses, which are built on stilts, are made of teak or split bamboo and have thatched roofs. They have shutters but no windows and deep verandas on which the family lives during the day. Usually a white-haired grandmother may be seen grating coconut for a curry or swinging the baby in a basket suspended from the ceiling.

I spent a great deal of time just walking around Bangkok. The scarcity of sidewalks and the heat do not make this the most pleasant pastime. But at daybreak it is cool, and that is when one may see the many yellow-robed monks with their bowls, begging for their daily ratio of rice. Those who give the food make a *wai* to thank the priest for the honor of being allowed to offer the food. This gesture, so common to Thailand, is as charming and graceful as it is courteous and respectful. The palms of the hands meet as in prayer under the face, with the head bowed. This may express greeting or gratitude or deference, and usually completely captivates a foreigner.

I used to walk through the shopping areas where there were rows of one-storied wooden buildings with shops completely open to the street. Here were Chinese tailors, jewelers, shoemakers, carpenters, barbers. Displays of hardware, china, brassware, fabrics, and baskets are on view to be examined and bargained for. It is impossible to pass a street without seeing the itinerant noodle maker who will serve you hot Chinese noodle soup and other Oriental delicacies. He carries his kitchen on a *hob* (a wooden pole with two heavy pots) suspended over his shoulder. He picks up his restaurant at a moment's notice and nimbly walks away with a brisk, graceful step, balancing his load. When I tired of strolling, I usually rode a *samlor*, a combination of bicycle and rickshaw, which is fast being displaced by taxis, automobiles, and buses. Everywhere there is motion, agitated and noisy, with horns honking and radios blaring.

My husband and I often went to the market which is a maze of wooden shanties where every imaginable article is displayed for sale. Meat hangs unrefrigerated from hooks, and on wide wooden planks are iced fish and dried fish, plucked poultry that is freshened periodically by a splash of cold water, strange sweetmeats, burlap sacks of various beans, betel nuts, eggs, fruits, vegetables, and spices of every description. There are also china, dry goods, clanking hardware, and even a stall with imported small electric appliances. The market teems with chattering buyers ready to leave the desired object unless their price is accepted and cautious sellers who know the most profitable moment to release the object.

Underneath all this apparent hubbub is the Thai's carefree acceptance of life so different from Western ideas of organization and efficiency. Our efforts to run our lives as we did at home left us fatigued and frustrated, but we observed that while there was no semblance to Western efficiency, there were no irritable Thai. When the water supply was cut off without apparent reason or warning, the Thai reaction was "It will come on soon." So then one could relax, chat, and pass the time of day pleasantly while waiting for the water to be turned on. Whatever it was that could keep the Siamese so calm, we secretly wished we could be infected by a little of it. Perhaps the most striking evidence of the difference in attitudes was our inability to get along with our cook.

You are probably wondering why we needed a cook, so perhaps a word of explanation is necessary before I go on. Most of the cooking in Thailand is done in an outbuilding, usually the servants' quarters, about fifty yards from the main house, in open, clay charcoal fire pots, and every item of food from the markets must be bargained for. To a newcomer without knowledge of the language and local know-how, a cook is indispensable. Whatever it was about us, whether pernicketiness or just plain bad luck, we never did well with any of the cooks we had. We were either "squeezed" on the food money, or forced to care for dozens of the cooks' ne'er-do-well relatives, or fed poorly cooked food, or just not fed enough. We felt put upon, deprived, and bullied. We even tried the do-it-yourself game and fanned the charcoal fires and did our own bargaining in the language we were learning, finally to come to the sad realization not only that were we doing a bad job of it, but also that we were accomplishing little else. Inevitably, we returned to the old-established way of doing things and hired a new cook. It turned out there were many who came and went, and the painful job of asking them to leave always arrived. Perhaps if some of the Eastern spirit had permeated our inflexible souls, we too could have looked the other way when trouble brewed and said with the Thai, "Never mind." And, as with all other troubles, these too would have passed.

Despite our kitchen problems, somehow the cooks worked magic, for by the time we were ready to leave Thailand, we had not only grown to love Siamese food but were eager to reproduce some of it for our friends at home. We had so completely lost our hearts in Siam that our travels through Europe on our way home were marked by the search for Oriental restaurants to assuage our homesickness. Imagine traipsing through Paris streets looking for rice and curry when *coq au vin* was available at the corner bistro.

There is nothing plain about Thai cooking. It is rich and highly seasoned, happily combining its Indian and Chinese origins. The Siamese dinner menu is conceived differently from our Western one. It must always include boiled rice, but the number of dishes served with the rice depends on the circumstances of the household as well as the importance of the occasion.

The rice is cooked without salt or fat so that it will contrast with the high seasoning of most of the other dishes accompanying it. It is served in a large covered bowl and holds a dignified place at the table. There is usually a curry of meat, fish, or fowl, and with the curry are served a few appetizing condiments. That in itself would be enough of a meal, but frequently there is more. Soup is served during the meal in little bowls with porcelain spoons. It is sometimes set on the table in a special charcoal tureen to keep it hot. Next come *kap khao,* or the side dishes to be eaten with rice. As you can imagine, one takes some rice and then a little of each of the other dishes.

Many Thai vegetables are not grown in America. In their salads the Thai use delicate water plants, young leafy shoots of trees, shrubs and vines, flowers and blossoms. Some of these are eaten dipped in vinegar or *nam pla* (fish sauce), or in egg batter and fried. However, cucumbers, tomatoes, scallions, lettuce, chili peppers, string beans, pumpkins and squashes resembling zucchini, and summer squash are commonly used in Thai cooking. Whatever they are, they are always arranged to please the eye. Cucumbers are scored lengthwise and sliced to look like cogwheels. Green onion tops are slit lengthwise and then dipped in ice water so they curl. Chili peppers are used both in cooking and as a garnish cut to look like flowers. The appearance of Siamese food is most important and is always commented upon by the Thai as much as the taste.

Dessert is always special. Unfortunately most Thai sweets are impossible to duplicate because the ingredients are not available in the West. There is a liquid sweet with lotus seeds or other nutty or bean-like food floating in a scented syrup. These are usually sweet-bland in taste, while other desserts are often very sweet. I have selected some that, with minor substitutions, may be easily made in the American kitchen. Fruit, however, is perhaps the most popular dessert. It is not served in our style in a large bowl but is peeled, sliced, and arranged decoratively on a platter. Pineapple, pomelo, mangosteen, rambutan, custard apple, mango, papaya, jackfruit, roseapple, durian, and many varieties of bananas and oranges are some of the delicious fruits grown in Thailand.

Formerly no eating utensils were used except porcelain soup spoons, food being eaten with the fingers as in India. However, every Thai is adept with chopsticks. Nowadays soup spoons and forks are commonly used, but not knives since ingredients for most dishes are cut into small pieces before they reach the table.

As for beverages, water, tea, or beer is served with meals. Coffee is drunk as a pick-me-up, strong and bitter, and cut with sweetened condensed milk. Usually only men indulge in alcoholic drinks, women preferring water or carbonated beverages. Before dinner, men often drink *mekong,* a local whiskey distilled by the government monopoly. This is a very mild spirit, a bit sweet, and rather like rye. It is usually mixed with soda. Milk is not available except the imported canned variety for babies only.

An important substitution I have made in these recipes is the use of soy sauce for the ubiquitous *nam pla* (fish sauce), a salty mixture that is added to just about everything. It may be obtained in some Oriental groceries, and, if such a shop is accessible to you, by all means use an equal amount of *nam pla* instead of the soy sauce listed in the recipes.

Thai dishes are not difficult to prepare. When I recall that in Thailand most of them are cooked in the traditional bowl-shaped frying pan on open charcoal stoves without the help of our modern kitchen devices, I marvel that they could be produced at all. Perhaps the most important kitchen tool of the Thai is the mortar and pestle with which chili peppers, spices, and other foods are pounded for long hours to reduce them to smooth, creamy substances. Even an electric blender cannot do as well.

Very few Thai dishes are baked. Their oven is a box made of sheet metal that sits on top of the open charcoal stove. Someone must be on hand to stoke the fire below and to keep the coals on top burning. Many foods are steamed, and the steamer is also a sheet-metal affair, cone-shaped, which sits atop the frying pan.

The recipes in this book contain no ingredients that are not available in the ordinary supermarket, and all of them have been adapted to the Western palate. You may find them a bit rich, but, since you won't be eating them every day, they are a welcome change from our comparatively bland cookery. After trying these dishes once or twice you will begin to sense what is the appropriate seasoning for you. My quantities are on the mild side, and, since there are no exact recipes for Thai food anyway, you can see that it is a matter of taste. Do not overlook the use of monosodium glutamate, referred to as m.s.g. In the Far East it sits next to the salt and pepper and is put into everything except desserts. Use from $\frac{1}{4}$ to $\frac{1}{2}$ teaspoon for 4 or 5 servings. Recipes in this book serve 4 or 5, unless otherwise noted, and most of them are a meal in themselves, served with rice, of course. All the oven temperatures are in Fahrenheit.

Keep your cutting board handy along with a sharp knife or two for there is much chopping to be done. Experiment and don't be afraid to do the unusual. The use of new herbs and spices will fill your house with appetizing odors and make meal time an exciting adventure.

A few words about Thai pronunciation may be helpful. Thai is a tonal language, which means that the inflection you give a word can change its meaning. Each syllable has a tone—middle, high, low, rising, or falling—which determines the meaning as much as the vowel and consonant sounds. Because this is too complicated for inclusion in a cookbook, I am merely listing a brief guide to pronunciation.

The consonant sounds are equivalent to the common English sounds with the following exceptions:

> g as in gill, kh as in kill, k between the two
> b as in bat, ph as in pat, p in between the two
> d as in dot, th as in tot, t in between the two
> ch as in cheese

Vowels are pronounced as follows:

> a as in father
> ae as in gang
> ai as in pie
> ao as in cow
> e as in get
> i as in me
> o as in dome
> u as in moon
> ü rather like the German ü

We have been back in the United States for some years now and we no longer suffer from homesickness for Siam, but Thai food has found a permanent place in our home. I hope this little book will make it a happy addition to your household.

I acknowledge my indebtedness to the following sources: *A History of South-East Asia* by D. G. E. Hall; *Conquest by Man* by

Paul Herrmann; *Perfumes and Spices* by A. Hyatt Verrill; "Mae Posop, the Rice Mother" by Phya Anuman Rajadhon in the *Journal of the Siam Society,* Vol. XLIII, Part I, August 1955; *Siam, An Account of the Country and the People* by P. A. Thompson; "National Consumption of Spices and Flavoring Oils Rose to Peak," by Michael Benson in *The New York Times,* January 9, 1961; and *Every Day Siamese Dishes* by Siphan Sonokul.

❧ Rice ❧
Khao

Rice is the mainstay of the Siamese diet and economy and is always served with salads, meats, poultry, fish, and sea food. Two-thirds of the Thai people earn a living from rice farming. They produce enough not only to feed themselves, but also to be one of the world's largest rice exporters. Rice farming is the greatest single contributor to national income, provides almost half of Thailand's export earnings, and is the major support of government revenues. When one hires a servant in Siam, it is customary to supply rice in addition to salary.

Besides its economic importance, rice has a deep psychological and cultural meaning for the Thai, according to Phya Anuman Rajadhon, distinguished Thai historian and scholar of the customs and traditions of his country. When a Siamese wishes to say he is hungry, he says, *"Hiu khao"* or "I'm hungry for rice." When he is eating, he says, *"Tan khao"* or "I'm eating rice." Even when he refers to food in general he uses the word *khao,* meaning rice.

There are many rituals and ceremonies that accompany rice farming, and, while some are losing their vitality with the passing of the older generation, others are practiced today. These observances are founded on the belief that there is a Rice Goddess or Rice Mother, *Mae Posop,* who, if properly worshiped and propitiated, will reward the farmer with prosperity and good health. For those who deny her, only poverty and sickness will be their end. It is said that she first came to reside in the land of the rice fields from Mount Meru, the home of the Hindu-Buddhist gods. Her journey over the Seven Seas and the Seven Mountain Ranges was long and tortuous. And on her heels came the many fish which today are still so plentiful in Siamese waters.

When rice plants begin to seed, the Thai expression is that the rice becomes pregnant. This is a crisis in the life of the plant, and therefore its *khwan* (spirit or soul) must be strengthened. It is believed that every living thing has a *khwan,* man, animal, and plant. When a person is ill, the *khwan* flees the body. Death means that the *khwan* does not return. During every crisis of life—birth, puberty, marriage—a ceremony is performed to strengthen this spirit. So for the pregnant Rice Mother an offering is made of

banana, citrus fruit, and sugar cane for her morning sickness. The farmer puts these foods in a bamboo basket which he hangs on a flag pole in the fields. This also serves as a warning to trespassers to keep their animals from treading on the rice plants. The farmer then takes a comb, toilet powder, and perfumed ointment and symbolically combs a rice plant, dabbing it with powder and ointment as though it were the Rice Mother herself. He prays that through his offerings the Rice Mother will thrive and not come to harm.

After the harvest, the rice missed in the reaping, representing the spirit of the Rice Mother, is gathered, with an entreaty to her to leave the field, where she may be in danger of prowling mice and birds, and to come and live in the barn instead. When the threshing is done, an offering of boiled duck eggs, sweets, and fruit is made to the Rice Mother. What rice paddy remains on the threshing floor is then put into a basket and called *Mae Posop's* rice. This is the spirit or essence of rice. Next a doll is made from rice straw and mixed with some of this paddy—as an image of the Rice Mother—and is kept in the barn with the paddy essence.

When the sowing of rice begins in the rainy season, the Rice Mother's essence is taken out of the barn and mixed with the paddy to be sown, to insure fertility. The doll is then ceremoniously destroyed.

Even when not directly concerned with the cultivation of rice, the Rice Mother must be propitiated. At the end of a meal children often raise their hands palm to palm in thanksgiving to the Rice Mother. It is said that her ire is incurred if, when eating, one allows grains of rice to fall to the floor, or if these grains are stepped on, or leftover rice is discarded. If one wishes to criticize the way rice has been cooked, one must beg the Rice Mother's pardon first and then politely make one's complaint. When fed to animals—and it is, by the way, the main source of food for cats, dogs, pigs, chickens, ducks, cows, and buffalo—rice must be offered in a container, not scattered on the ground, for the Rice Mother's wrath may be incurred. The threatening danger is that she will leave the offender, and only bad luck will surround him without her.

In the Buddha's life there is an interesting story in which rice plays an important part. It was the time when he was following the path of asceticism and was abstaining from food in his search for spiritual enlightenment. A young woman, Sujata, daughter of a wealthy cattle owner, was pregnant and wished for a son. She made a vow to a tree deity that if he would let her child be a boy, she would prepare for the god an elaborate rice porridge. Since her child was a boy, she kept her promise. First a thousand cows were milked, and this milk was fed to five hundred cows. Then the milk of five hundred cows was fed to two hundred fifty cows, and so on until a highly concentrated milk was obtained from eight cows. In a golden pot this rich milk was mixed with rice and other ingredients (I wish I knew what they were!). During the cooking the god Indra got a whiff of this wonderful concoction and sprinkled heavenly spices into the pot, which so enhanced the porridge that it is said its taste and aroma were incredibly exquisite.

Meanwhile, in the deep forest, the Buddha was sitting under the same banyan tree to which Sujata made her vow. She brought the porridge to him in a golden bowl, believing him to be the tree god. After six years of asceticism but still without achieving nirvana, the Buddha decided to follow the Middle Path in search of absolute truth. He accepted and ate the food. He then took the empty bowl to the river's edge and, wishing for a sign that he would some day achieve enlightenment, told himself that if this noble condition were to be his in the future then the bowl would float upstream. He flung the bowl into the water, and, miracle of miracles, it did float upstream. Then it sank to the bottom to join the golden bowls which belonged to the three previous Buddhas.

Boiled Rice
Khao

The Thai like their rice white and polished, and the brown portion is discarded or fed to livestock. The rice is washed several times before cooking which further robs it of its nutrients. Leaving out the washing process, however, the following is a recipe for Thai boiled rice. Note that no salt or butter is added.

1 *cup rice*	1¾ *cups cold water*

Combine rice and water, bring to a boil, cover, and cook for 5 minutes. Then reduce to low heat and cook for 20 minutes longer or until all the water is absorbed. The rice should look dry and flaky.

A really foolproof and simple way to get the same result is the following:

1 *cup rice*	2 *cups boiling water*

Combine rice and boiling water in a covered baking dish. Put it into the oven and bake for an hour at 350 degrees. After an hour reduce heat to 225 degrees and the rice will keep warm and flaky until it is served. The added convenience of being able to serve the rice in the dish in which it is baked makes this method superior to the Thai one.

In northeastern Thailand, as in Laos, glutinous rice is grown and preferred to ordinary rice. This sticky rice is soaked for several hours in water to make it swell and then steamed in a cone-shaped basket. The basket stands on the table near one's plate, and the rice is picked out with the hand and kneaded into a ball. It is eaten with no curry or other food over it. In central Thailand sticky rice is cooked in coconut cream and served alongside sliced ripe mangoes as a dessert. This is one of the most wonderful desserts I have ever eaten.

Fried Rice

Khao Phat

The Siamese always prepare more rice than they need for any one meal, so there is always some left for a *khao phat,* should someone get hungry. This dish makes an excellent lunch and is so flexible that it can be combined with whatever you happen to have on hand. Leftover meat, canned or fresh shrimp, slices of uncooked chicken, pork, or beef may be used. The ginger and garlic, however, are indispensable. Some cooks add a bit of tomato sauce to give color. When we traveled by train around Siam, we were served *khao phat* wrapped in a large green banana leaf, just as warm as toast and very tasty.

3 *tablespoons butter*	*both green and white parts*
2 *teaspoons minced fresh or*	5–6 *cups cooked rice*
crystallized ginger	*salt and pepper to taste*
1 *clove garlic, crushed*	*m.s.g.*
½ *cup thinly sliced pork*	2 *eggs*
½ *dozen shrimp, shelled*	*slices of cucumber, tomato, and*
and deveined	*scallion for garnish*
½ *cup chopped scallions,*	

In a large frying pan melt butter and stir-fry the ginger and garlic. Add pork and stir-fry until well done. Add shrimp and sauté until tender. Stir in chopped scallions. Add rice and stir-fry until rice is heated through. Add seasonings. Crack the eggs right over the rice and stir-fry until they are well mixed. Serve garnished with slices of cucumber, tomato, and scallions. Fresh red chili peppers are also used as a garnish, but radishes make a good substitute.

Many cooks make a thin omelet with an additional 2 eggs, well beaten and seasoned with salt and pepper, fried thin in a large frying pan, then cut into ½-inch strips, and arranged decoratively with the vegetables over the *khao phat*. This makes the meal even more hearty and may be made while the rice keeps warm in the pan.

❀ Curry ❀
Kaeng Phet

Curry is one of Thailand's favorite dishes, but in the Thai language *kari* (curry) refers, however, to only one of many combinations of spices. It contains turmeric or saffron among other things and can be recognized by its yellow color. The Thai housewife blends in a mortar and pestle many other combinations of spices, each with its own name. For our purposes we can call them all curry. In its many forms, curry is common to India and all of Southeast Asia, including Malaya, Indonesia, Laos, Cambodia, and Burma.

The consumption of spices is as old as civilization. Most of the spices we know today were used in ancient Egypt, China, India, and Sumeria, not only to add zest to food, but also to preserve meat and to conceal the evidence of that already spoiled. Spices have always been greatly valued. Until modern times many of the best known, for example nutmeg and cloves, came only from Southeast Asia. Men sailed uncharted seas swarming with Malay and Chinese pirates, dared the lands of savage headhunters, ripped their vessels on hidden reefs; and died in the lonely seas in quest of these spices.

In ancient times people utilized spices in many more ways than we do today. The Egyptians used spices and other substances in the preparation of their mummies. Spices played an important role in the making of perfumes, and in passages of the Bible we find scents referred to as "spicery." One of the many recipes for making holy anointing oil given to Moses by God was exceedingly spicy:

Moreover the Lord spake unto Moses, saying, Take thou also unto thee the chief spices, of flowing myrrh five hundred shekels, and of sweet cinnamon half so much, even two hundred and fifty, and of sweet calamus two hundred fifty, and of cassia five hundred, after the shekel of the sanctuary, and of olive oil an hin: and thou shalt make it an holy anointing oil, a perfume compounded after the art of the perfumer: it shall be an holy anointing oil. And thou shalt anoint therewith the tent of meeting, and the ark of testimony, and the table and all the vessels thereof, and the candlestick and the vessels thereof, and the altar of incense, and the altar of burnt offering with all the vessels thereof, and the laver and the base thereof. And thou shalt sanctify them, that they may be most holy: whatsoever toucheth them shall be holy.

— EXODUS

Using more familiar units of measure, this recipe would read 18 pounds of myrrh, nine pounds of cinnamon, nine pounds of sweet calamus, 18 pounds of cassia (Chinese cinnamon), mixed with 1⅓ gallons of olive oil. The quantity and fragrance of this paste must have been staggering, for it covered quite a bit of territory.

As early as 300 B.C. caravans went from Europe to the Middle East and then to China, taking spices from Levantine exchanges to trade for silk. Roman ships sailed to Asia for spices, and the number of Roman coins found in far-off places tells us that the trade of those days must have been pretty lively indeed.

We owe a great debt to the Arab caravans for it was they who transported pepper, cloves, cardamon, and nutmeg across Asia. The military expeditions of the crusades brought thousands of Europeans into contact with the Arab Orient and its wonders, and spices became an indispensable ingredient in European life. Venice became the great market of world trade. Cloves and nutmeg from the Moluccas, cinnamon from Ceylon, pepper from Malabar, myrrh from Arabia, and ginger from India came to Venice and were passed on north and west.

Spices in Europe were as valuable as gold. Pepper was deemed to be the greatest of royal gifts and was worth its weight in gold. Taxes could be paid in pepper. Spices were also widely used in the making of medicines, and a strong tasting medicine was believed to have greater curative powers than a pleasant tasting one. Spices, of course, were vital in cooking too. From a 14th-century

German cookbook, Paul Herrmann in *Conquest by Man* gives two recipes for spice cookery:

Fish Pasty. To make a fish pasty, first scale the fish and skin them when they come to the boil. Chop them into small pieces. Mix in chopped parsley and sage, and add plenty of pepper and ginger, mint and saffron. Moisten the whole mixture with wine. Make a thin, stiff dough and put the fish into it. Pour the wine over them, and cover them with a thin layer of dough all over. Make a hole in the top and place a lid of dough over this hole. Then bake. The same can be done with chicken, as well as meat or game, eels or birds.

Stuffed Eels. Take fresh eels and clean the slime off with ashes. Loosen the skin at the head and pull it back to the tail. Chop sage and parsley and add plenty of ground ginger, pepper, aniseed, and salt. Throw this over the eels and pull up the skin again. Sprinkle the eels with salt, roast thoroughly on a wooden spit, and serve.

This style of cooking hardly suits our modern methods. "Take plenty of" probably is sufficiently accurate so that such seasoning must have produced peppy concoctions. The reason for this apparently was that it was impossible to feed livestock during the winter. The animals were slaughtered and salted down at the onset of the cold. A diet of salted food being rather monotonous, huge quantities of spices were used to make meats palatable.

The cost of spices made them a luxury even for the rich, and great effort went into the spice business. As the demand increased. it was clear that the only way to lower the price was to eliminate some of the many hands through which the spices passed out of Asia through Arabia to Europe. By the end of the 15th century European states began to look for an ocean route to the places where these spices grew. Politics also affected the spice trade because the Ottoman Empire had come to hold a monopoly on eastern Mediterranean trade. It became an urgent necessity then for Europe to break this monopoly by finding new sources of all these spices.

European geographers generally thought that you could not

sail around the Dark Continent. They believed that the Indian Ocean was an inland sea and that somehow Africa joined India. However, Arab geographers thought it was possible to sail around Africa, and what is more, they claimed that an Arab vessel had already rounded the Cape of Good Hope in 1420.

The Portuguese were the first Europeans to venture expeditions around Africa, and it was Prince Henry the Navigator, intrigued by the notion that the earth was round, who was responsible for stimulating the Portuguese to mastery of the Eastern seas. It was Henry, though he never went to sea himself, who brought personal pressure upon his captains to sail west and south, in spite of the nightmarish tales of sea monsters, gelatinous seas, and infernal abysses waiting to drag down unsuspecting ships. In 1446 a Portuguese ship reached Cape Verde to discover lush tropical vegetation and the changing direction of the African coastline from southwest to southeast.

Prince Henry died before he achieved his goal, and it was not until 1487 when two expeditions were dispatched by the Portuguese Crown that his dream was to materialize. One went by land to India and Abyssinia, and the other, led by Bartholomew Diaz, by sea southward and around the Dark Continent. After many months of turbulent seas, spoiled supplies, and a frightened crew, Diaz sighted land which turned out to be the southernmost tip of Africa. He called it the Cape of Good Hope because a sea route to India had at last been proved to exist. It was Vasco da Gama, another Portuguese, who successfully pressed on into the Indian Ocean. The Portuguese had superiority over the Arabs in both shipbuilding and seamanship, and it was not long before they expanded their power and influence in the East. The European market moved from Venice to Lisbon. The Portuguese Christians were not only able to serve God by fighting Islam, but also to wrest from the Moors the monopoly of the spice trade.

The Spaniards too had made an effort to take part in the

spice trade. Queen Isabella sent Columbus in search of the Spice Islands and especially Cathay, the land of the great Kubla Khan. But instead of the spices he sought, he found gold and other treasures and later Spaniards found two new spices in the New World. In Jamaica strange trees, gnarled and twisted, grew wild over vast areas and bore a berry which when dried tasted like a blend of cloves, cinnamon, and nutmeg. We call it allspice. They also found a pungent replacement for the pepper plants of the Asian jungles. Everywhere in Central and South America and the West Indies they found the natives cultivating a plant bearing fiery-tasting pods of varying size, shape, and color, which they called chili. One small piece of these pods brought tears to the eyes of a Spaniard. These chilies make what we know as cayenne pepper. Unlike the allspice which grows only in the Western hemisphere, chilies have been successfully planted all over the world. The Thai as well as other peoples of Southeast Asia, India, and Africa are devotees of this hot plant.

The Portuguese spice monopoly did not last for long because both Holland and Britain entered competition for the trade. In the struggle the Dutch gained vast possessions in Indonesia, and the British acquired control of India, Ceylon, and Singapore. For almost a century the British and Dutch competed, squabbled, and warred fiercely for control of the trade and sources of cinnamon, cloves, and nutmeg.

The American colonies also had a hand in the spice trade long before they achieved their independence, and the so-called China trade paid them tremendous profits. The rise of the American merchant marine goes back to this period. A New England shipmaster is said to have discovered pepper in Sumatra and brought home a cargo load. Five hundred tons of pepper were exported to Europe from New England in 1805. In 1826 a huge cargo of cloves and pepper overflowed U.S. markets, and the surplus was traded with Cuba for sugar. By this time the monopolies were gone, the saturation point had been reached, and, with the expansion of world trade, the spice trade became less and less important.

Today, while spices may not be one of the world's leading commodities, they continue to increase in their importance to the American housewife. By 1960 Americans spent more than $35,000,000 for spices and flavoring oil, representing approximately 250,000,000 pounds compared with 150,000,000 ten years ago. We go to our local supermarket and find every known spice from far-off places, attractively boxed or bottled and costing only a few cents. In Thailand, as in other places in Southeast Asia, these same spices are to be found in open markets, dried but not ground, heaped in mounds, to be bargained for by the handful and wrapped for the customer in an old newspaper.

Curry Pastes
Khrung Kaeng

A Thai housewife takes the "right" amounts of each spice without the help of a measuring spoon and pounds them together in a mortar and pestle. There are no recipes for these combinations—instinct, taste, and past experience are the measures. If you do not own a mortar and pestle, a good pepper grinder does an efficient job on the seeds of coriander, cardamon, and caraway. Measure them after they are ground as they tend to increase in bulk. After pounding, the Thai blend their spices with *kapi,* a paste made of shrimp. I have found anchovy paste and vinegar work almost as well. When preparing curry, for each pound of meat use approximately 2 teaspoons of curry paste and 1 cup of liquid (stock, coconut cream, milk, etc.). Because both fish and fowl take less time to cook than meat, the liquid should be reduced by about half. You may prepare the paste in advance to have on hand when you need it. Stored in a small jar in the refrigerator, it will keep for weeks.

CURRY PASTE FOR MEAT:

1 tablespoon freshly grated nutmeg

½ teaspoon ground cloves

1 teaspoon mace

10 cardamon pods (remove seeds and grind) Yield is approximately 1 teaspoon. 1 teaspoon cardamon powder may be substituted

¼ teaspoon cayenne pepper (or to taste)

2 tablespoons ground coriander seed

½ teaspoon ground caraway seed

1½ teaspoons paprika

2 tablespoons anchovy paste

2 teaspoons vinegar

Combine all dry ingredients. Add the anchovy paste and vinegar and mix well. Keep in a small airtight jar.

CURRY PASTE FOR POULTRY AND SEA FOOD:

1 tablespoon ground coriander seed

1 tablespoon ground caraway seed

1 teaspoon turmeric

1 teaspoon black pepper

¼ teaspoon cayenne pepper (or to taste)

½ teaspoon freshly grated nutmeg

2 tablespoons anchovy paste

2 teaspoons vinegar

Combine the dry ingredients and add the anchovy paste and vinegar as above.

Coconut Cream for Curry

In a land where coconut trees are abundant, the Thai use large amounts of coconut cream in their cookery. They shred the meat of fresh coconuts and soak it in water, and the resulting white liquid is used in cooking much as we use stock. Our packaged shredded coconut cannot be substituted. It is too sweet and suited only for desserts. It did not seem to me practical for most of these dishes to grate fresh coconuts even when they were available fresh when needed. So I tried to find a good substitute. I checked with Thai friends in the United States who told me they used cow's milk, sweet cream, or buttermilk. However, when I suggested sour cream they approved enthusiastically as soon as they tasted a curry made with it.

I know there is always a cook who is both enterprising and energetic, and for just that one I offer here the way to prepare coconut cream for a curry. In a saucepan combine:

> 3 *cups freshly grated coconut*　　3 *cups water*
> 　(*1 large or 2 small coconuts*)

Bring to a boil. Let stand for about half an hour or until cooled. Press all the liquid from the coconut using a strainer and discard the pulp. Use this coconut cream in place of the stock in all curry recipes (except the shrimp curry) and, of course, omit the sour cream.

Since shrimp curry cooks for such a short time, use only 1½ cups water to 3 cups grated coconut. Keep in mind in all these recipes that after cooking, the liquid should reduce to about 1 cupful. Add more water if needed, or boil off some if you have too much.

If you use cow's milk, evaporated milk, sweet cream, or buttermilk, remember it is used in place of the stock, just as you would use the coconut cream. Any of these will produce a very good curry.

Whichever way you decide to make it, keep in mind that Thai curry is not thickened, so don't be surprised to find the sauce thin. Sour cream does have a thickening effect, but not so the coconut cream. Also experiment with the mixture. If the curry seems mild to you, add more paste or chili peppers. Approach the matter as a Thai cook would. Each family has its own taste which the cook is obliged to satisfy. And, of course, be sure to have some condiments on hand to be served with your curry. Choose at least three from the list below.

Condiments Served with Curry

Rice is heaped on the plate first, then the curry over it. The condiments may be sprinkled on top or kept in separate mounds.

sliced bananas
salted peanuts
grated coconut
chutney (page 94)
minced onions, crisply fried and salted
chopped scallions
cucumber relish (page 58)
pineapple chunks
chopped water chestnuts
sliced cystallized ginger
sliced hard-boiled eggs

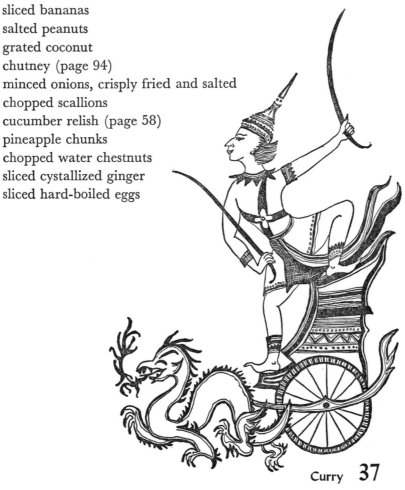

Meat Curry
Kaeng Nüa

4 *cloves garlic, crushed*
3 *tablespoons salad oil*
2 *pounds stewing beef cut*
into ½-inch cubes
1 *cup chopped onions*
4 *teaspoons curry paste for*
meat (page 35)
2 *cups stock (page 44)*
1 *teaspoon salt*
m.s.g.
1 *cup sour cream (page 35*
coconut cream in place of
sour cream)

Brown the garlic in hot oil. Add the meat and stir-fry over high heat until well browned. Add onions and stir-fry until they are golden. Stir in curry paste. Add stock, salt, and m.s.g. Bring to a boil. Then cover and simmer over a low fire for 2 hours or until liquid is reduced to less than a cupful. Stir in the sour cream until heated, but do not boil.

Leftover beef and even lamb or pork may be used in this recipe. Reduce the quantity of stock to one cupful and cook only about thirty minutes. Results are almost as good as starting from scratch.

Moslem Curry

Kaeng Masaman

4 *cloves garlic, crushed*
3 *tablespoons salad oil*
2 *pounds stewing beef cut into ½-inch cubes*
1 *cup chopped onions*
4 *teaspoons curry paste for meat (page 35)*
2 *cups stock (page 44)*
8 *bay leaves*
1 *whole dried chili pepper (remove seeds)*

1 *tablespoon brown sugar*
1 *2-inch cinnamon stick*
1 *teaspoon salt*
m.s.g.
1 *cup sour cream (page 35 coconut cream in place of sour cream)*
¼ *cup chopped peanuts*

Brown garlic in hot oil. Add the beef and brown over high heat, stirring frequently. Add the onions and brown. Stir in the curry paste. Add stock, bay leaves, chili pepper, brown sugar, cinnamon stick, salt, and m.s.g. Bring to a boil. Then cover and simmer for 2 hours. Liquid should reduce to about ¾ of a cup. Remove the bay leaves, chili pepper, and cinnamon stick. Stir in the sour cream. Do not boil. Serve the curry sprinkled with chopped peanuts.

Duck Curry

Kaeng Pet

A cut-up 3–4 pound duck may be cooked in the same way as the beef in the Moslem Curry. Use only 1½ cups of stock and simmer for an hour or until duck is tender.

Chicken Curry

Kaeng Kai

2 cloves garlic, crushed

3 tablespoons butter or salad oil

1 3–4 pound chicken cut up into serving pieces

1 large onion, chopped

4 teaspoons curry paste for poultry (page 35)

1½ cups stock (page 44)

½ teaspoon grated lime rind

1 tablespoon sweet basil

1 whole dried chili pepper (remove seeds)

1 teaspoon salt

m.s.g.

1 cup sour cream (page 35 coconut cream in place of sour cream)

Brown garlic in the hot oil. Then brown chicken over high heat. Add onions and brown. Stir in curry paste. Add stock, lime rind, sweet basil, chili pepper, salt, and m.s.g. Bring to a boil. Cover and simmer for about an hour or until chicken is tender. Remove the pepper. Stir in sour cream. Do not allow the cream to boil.

Shrimp Curry

Kaeng Kung

1 *clove garlic, crushed*
3 *tablespoons butter*
4 *teaspoons curry paste for sea food (page 35)*
2 *pounds shrimp, shelled and deveined*
2 *slices lemon*
½ *cup stock (page 44)*
1 *bay leaf*
1 *whole dried chili pepper (remove seeds)*
½ *teaspoon salt*
m.s.g.
1 *cup sour cream (page 35 coconut cream in place of sour cream)*

Melt butter in a large frying pan. Add garlic and curry paste and stir-fry for a minute. Add shrimp and sauté over low heat, first on one side then on the other until pink. Add lemon slices, stock, bay leaf, pepper, salt, and m.s.g. Stir. Cover and simmer for 15 minutes over low heat. Add sour cream and serve as soon as cream is heated.

✤ Soups ✤
Kaeng Chüt

Thai soups are very Chinese in character with perhaps more seasoning. Some are so hearty they may almost be a meal in themselves. A Thai dinner always includes soup, but unlike our custom, soup is never served before the meal. It is eaten along with the other dishes or even after. Small individual covered bowls are ideal, or a soup tureen set in the center of the table may be used. If Chinese mushrooms are not available, fresh, canned, or the large dried European ones may be used just as well. The soup should always be served with a touch of green floating on its surface and a bit of red, if hot red chili peppers are palatable to you.

Soup Stock

3 *pounds chicken backs and*
  necks
3 *quarts water*
1 *large onion quartered*
3–4 *celery tops*

1 *bay leaf*
1 *teaspoon salt*
6 *peppercorns*
m.s.g.

Combine these ingredients in a large pot, bring to a boil, and simmer covered for 2 hours. Strain the soup, saving some of the choice bits of chicken to be used in the recipes that follow.

Chicken and Mushroom Soup
Kaeng Kai Kap Het

1 *tablespoon butter*
1 *clove garlic, crushed*
½ *teaspoon ground coriander*
¼ *teaspoon pepper*
2 *teaspoons soy sauce*
½ *cup thinly sliced cooked*
  (or uncooked) chicken
3½ *cups stock (page 44)*
¼ *teaspoon salt*
m.s.g.
¾ *cup sliced mushrooms*
chopped scallion greens

Melt butter. Add garlic, coriander, and pepper and stir for a few seconds. Stir in soy sauce. Add chicken and stir-fry one minute. Add stock, salt, and m.s.g. and bring to the boiling point. Then simmer for 15 minutes. Add mushrooms and simmer for 5 minutes longer. Serve garnished with the scallion greens.

Laotian Mushroom Soup
Kaeng Het Bot

Using the recipe above, leave out the chicken and add one cup of tiny button mushrooms to the seasoned broth.

Laotian Cabbage Soup
Kaeng Kalampi

1 *tablespoon butter*	3½ *cups stock (page 44)*
1 *clove garlic, crushed*	¼ *teaspoon salt*
½ *teaspoon ground coriander*	*m.s.g.*
¼ *teaspoon pepper*	2 *cups thinly sliced cabbage*
2 *teaspoons soy sauce*	*chopped scallion greens*

Melt butter. Add garlic, coriander, and pepper. Stir for a few seconds. Stir in soy sauce. Add stock, salt, and m.s.g. and bring to the boiling point. Then simmer for 15 minutes. Add cabbage and simmer for 5 or 10 minutes or until cabbage is tender. Garnish with the scallion greens.

Shrimp, Pork, and Mushroom Soup
Kaeng Kung Kap Het

1 *teaspoon butter*	3½ *cups stock (page 44)*
1 *clove garlic, crushed*	¼ *teaspoon salt*
½ *teaspoon ground coriander*	*m.s.g.*
¼ *teaspoon pepper*	1 *dozen medium shrimp,*
2 *teaspoons soy sauce*	*either fresh or canned*
½ *cup thinly sliced raw (or*	½ *cup mushrooms*
cooked) pork	*chopped scallion greens*

Melt butter. Add garlic, coriander, and pepper. Stir for a few seconds. Stir in soy sauce. Add pork and stir-fry until browned. Add stock, salt, and m.s.g. and bring to the boiling point. Then simmer for 15 minutes or until pork is done. Add shrimp and mushrooms and simmer for 5 minutes longer or until shrimp are pink. Serve garnished with the scallion greens.

Fish Balls and Mushroom Soup
Kaeng Luk Chin

½ *pound fresh fish boned,*
  skinned, and ground
1 *teaspoon ground coriander*
1 *clove garlic, crushed*
½ *teaspoon pepper*
¼ *teaspoon salt*
m.s.g.
4 *cups stock (page 44)*
1½ *cups unpeeled, thinly*
  sliced zucchini
½ *cup sliced mushrooms*
1 *tablespoon soy sauce*
chopped parsley

Put the fish through a food grinder. Add the coriander, garlic, pepper, salt, and m.s.g. Mix well and form balls the size of marbles. Bring stock to the boiling point. Add the fish balls and simmer 5 minutes. Add the zucchini and mushrooms and cook a few minutes longer or until tender. Season with soy sauce and add more salt and pepper if needed. Serve garnished with chopped parsley.

Bamboo Shoots and Pork Soup
Kaeng No Mai

This soup is also common in Laos.

2 tablespoons butter or oil
1 clove garlic, crushed
½ teaspoon coriander
¼ teaspoon pepper
2 teaspoons soy sauce
⅔ cup thinly sliced raw (or cooked) pork
1 tablespoon sugar
4 cups stock (page 44)
¼ teaspoon salt
m.s.g.
⅔ cup canned, drained bamboo shoots, sliced thin
watercress or chopped scallion greens

Melt butter. Add garlic, coriander, and pepper. Stir in soy sauce. Add pork and stir-fry until brown. Add sugar, stock, salt, and m.s.g. and simmer for 15 minutes or until pork is done. Add bamboo shoots and cook 2 minutes longer. Garnish with the watercress or scallion greens.

Shrimp, Pork, Chicken, and Cucumber Soup

Kaeng Ron

Here is the heartiest of the soups. Serve it with Fried Rice (page 25) or one of the salads and you have an unusual luncheon.

2 tablespoons butter

½ teaspoon ground coriander

¼ teaspoon pepper

1 clove garlic, crushed

½ cup thinly sliced onion

2 teaspoons soy sauce

¼ cup thinly sliced raw (or cooked) lean pork

¼ cup thinly sliced raw (or cooked) chicken

4 cups stock (page 44)

¼ teaspoon salt

m.s.g.

¼ cup sliced mushrooms

¼ cup cooked shrimp

1½ cups cucumbers, quartered, then thinly sliced

2 eggs, beaten

chopped parsley

Melt butter. Add coriander, pepper, garlic, and onions. Cook over low heat stirring frequently until onions are translucent. Stir in soy sauce. Add pork and chicken and stir-fry over high heat until meat is brown. Add stock, salt, and m.s.g. Bring to a boil. Simmer for 20 minutes or until meat is done. Add mushrooms, shrimp, and cucumbers and simmer 5 minutes longer. Add the eggs a little at a time, stirring constantly. Serve garnished with the parsley. Serves 4–6.

Duck and Chestnut Soup

Pet Dom Kap Kaolat

1 *duck about 2½ pounds (substitute half larger duck)*	1 *bay leaf*
	1 *large onion quartered*
	1 *teaspoon salt*
4 *quarts water*	

Bone the duck and boil only the carcass with the other **ingredients** for 1½ hours. Strain, cool stock, and skim off fat.

3 *tablespoons salad oil*	*uncooked meat from the duck cut into ½-inch pieces*
1 *clove garlic, crushed*	
2 *teaspoons ground coriander*	2 *cups shelled sliced chestnuts*
1 *teaspoon pepper*	*chopped chives or watercress*
m.s.g.	

In a large pot brown the garlic and add the coriander, pepper, and duck meat, stirring frequently over a high flame until well browned. Add the strained stock and chestnuts and bring to a boil. Then cover and simmer for 15 minutes or until meat and nuts are tender. Serve garnished with chopped chives or watercress. Serves 6–8.

Sour Shrimp Soup

Dom Yam Kung

The "sour" soups are typically Thai. They usually contain lemon grass and *makrut* (Kaffir lime) leaves, both of which contribute the tart flavor but are hard to come by in this country. You find bits of red chili floating on top of the *dom yam* too, and the combination makes the unsuspecting eater cry and cough. These recipes are tame. Go easy on the lemon juice and cayenne. Then add as much as you can stand and you will have approximately the genuine article.

1 *pound shrimp, shelled and deveined*	1 *teaspoon soy sauce*
4½ *cups stock (page 44)*	2 *tablespoons lemon juice (or to taste)*
1 *clove garlic, crushed*	*dash of cayenne*
½ *teaspoon ground coriander*	*salt to taste*
2 *bay leaves*	*m.s.g.*
2 *lemon slices*	*chopped scallion greens*

Combine all the ingredients except the shrimp. Bring to a boil and simmer for 15 minutes. Add the cleaned shrimp and cook 10 minutes longer or until the shrimp are done. Serve garnished with finely chopped scallion greens.

Sour Pork Soup
Dom Yam Mu

½ *pound lean pork*
1 *clove garlic, crushed*
5 *cups stock (page 44)*
½ *teaspoon ground coriander*
2 *bay leaves*
2 *lemon slices*

m.s.g.
1 *teaspoon soy sauce*
2 *tablespoons lemon juice*
dash of cayenne
salt to taste
chopped parsley

Combine pork, garlic, stock, coriander, bay leaves, lemon slices, and m.s.g. Bring to the boiling point and then simmer for half an hour or until pork is well done. Cool. Remove meat and cut into thin slices. Strain stock and remove excess fat. Add all the other ingredients. Return meat to stock and reheat. Serve garnished with finely chopped parsley.

Sour Beef Soup
Dom Yam Nüa

½ *pound beef cut into*
   small thin slices
1 *clove garlic, crushed*
5 *cups stock (page 44)*
2 *bay leaves*
2 *lemon slices*
m.s.g.

½ *teaspoon coriander*
1 *teaspoon soy sauce*
2 *tablespoons lemon juice (or*
   to taste)
dash of cayenne
salt to taste
chopped chives

Combine beef, garlic, stock, bay leaves, lemon slices, and m.s.g. Bring to a boil and simmer over low heat for 1 hour or until meat is tender. Add the remaining ingredients and serve garnished with chopped chives.

❧ Salads ❧

YAM

The Thai *yam* is equivalent to our salad, but of course it is customarily eaten with rice as are all the other dishes. Some of the *yams* are pretty substantial, and, from our point of view, may be used by themselves as luncheons, since they contain meat or fish and sometimes even a starch, as well as uncooked vegetables and fruits. They are usually garnished with coriander leaves and red chili peppers. Parsley and radishes may be substituted. All are delicious and not a bit strange to the Western palate.

Grapefruit Salad
Yam Som-O

In Thailand this is made with pomelo, a relative of the grapefruit. The pomelo is shredded and mixed with the other ingredients.

2 *grapefruits*	1½ *teaspoons soy sauce*
lettuce leaves	2 *tablespoons lemon juice*
½ *cup packaged shredded*	3 *tablespoons water*
coconut	1 *clove garlic, crushed*
2 *teaspoons sugar*	¼ *cup minced onion*

Peel and section grapefruit. Then remove membrane around each section and arrange segments on lettuce leaves in individual salad plates. Chill. Toast coconut in oven until light brown. Mix sugar, soy sauce, lemon juice and water together in a cup. Brown onion and garlic in hot oil. Drain on absorbent paper. Mix together sauce, coconut and onions and pour over grapefruit.

Galloping Horses
Ma Ho

Here is a delicious orange salad.

4 *navel oranges*
1 *tablespoon salad oil*
1 *clove garlic, crushed*
¼ *cup minced raw pork*
1 *tablespoon finely chopped*
  peanuts
1 *teaspoon sugar*
1 *tablespoon soy sauce*
1 *tablespoon water*
dash salt and cayenne pepper
m.s.g.
parsley sprigs

Peel and section oranges. Then remove membrane around each section and arrange segments on lettuce leaves. Chill. Brown garlic in the salad oil. Add pork and stir-fry until brown. When pork is done add everything else. Stir-fry until well mixed and pour over oranges. Garnish with sprigs of parsley.

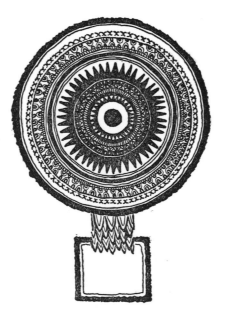

Beef and Zucchini Salad

Yam Nüa Kap Makhüa

½ *pound cold thin slices of*
rare to medium roast beef

2 *cups shredded lettuce*
1 *cup cooked sliced zucchini*

DRESSING:

1 *clove garlic, crushed*
2 *teaspoons soy sauce*
½ *cup lemon juice*
4 *teaspoons sugar*

salt and pepper
m.s.g.
chopped parsley

Slice unpared zucchini and cook in ½ inch of boiling water for a few minutes until tender. Drain and cool. Arrange beef slices on a platter. Cover with shredded lettuce and zucchini.

Combine the ingredients for the dressing. Mix until sugar dissolves. Pour over the meat and vegetables. Garnish with parsley.

Beef, Tomato, and Cucumber Salad

Yam Nüa Kap Mukoethet Lae Daengkwa

Substitute tomatoes and cucumbers for the zucchini in the above recipe.

Cucumber Boats

Yam Nüa Lae Daengkwa

2 *cucumbers*
½ *cup crisply fried minced*
  onion
½ *cup shredded slices of*

rare to medium roast beef
lettuce leaves
parsley sprigs

DRESSING:

1 *clove garlic, crushed*
4 *teaspoons dried mint*
½ *teaspoon soy sauce*
2 *tablespoons lemon juice*

1 *teaspoon sugar*
salt and pepper
m.s.g.

Pare cucumbers. Cut in half crosswise. Then cut in half lengthwise. With a spoon, scoop out seeds and pulp to form a boat. Mince two onions and fry until brown in a tablespoon of hot salad oil. Drain and measure out ½ cupful. Combine ingredients for the dressing and stir until sugar dissolves. Add the onion and beef. Fill the cucumber boats. Arrange them on lettuce leaves and garnish with sprigs of parsley.

Cucumber Relish
Yam Daengkwa

2 *cups cucumbers, sliced*
  paper thin

¼ *cup minced onion*

DRESSING:

1½ *tablespoons chopped*
   scallion greens
⅛ *cup lemon juice*
4 *teaspoons soy sauce*

¼ *teaspoon pepper*
1 *teaspoon sugar*
m.s.g.

Combine the cucumbers, onion, and scallions in a bowl. Make the dressing and add it to the cucumbers. Be sure to mix the relish well before serving.

Shrimp and Watercress Salad
Yam Kung

1 *pound shrimp*
1 *bunch watercress*

lettuce leaves

DRESSING:

2 *tablespoons minced scal-*
  lions
1 *clove garlic, crushed*
1 *tablespoon soy sauce*
¼ *cup salad oil*
¼ *cup lemon juice*

2 *teaspoons sugar*
1 *tablespoon water*
salt and pepper
m.s.g.
2 *tablespoons chopped pea-*
  nuts (optional)

Boil shrimp 10–15 minutes, shell, and devein. Arrange the watercress on the lettuce leaves, cooked shrimp on top of both. Combine the dressing ingredients and pour over the salad.

Great Salad

Yai Yam

Here is a large hearty salad suitable for a luncheon. It is all cold except for the vermicelli dish that must be made just before serving.

½ pound sliced cooked pork

½ pound sliced cooked chicken

1 pound cooked shrimp

2 sliced cucumbers

2 large tomatoes, sliced

lettuce leaves

DRESSING for the above to be passed at the table:

¼ cup lemon juice

¼ cup vinegar

2 teaspoons soy sauce

4 teaspoons sugar

salt and pepper

m.s.g.

Using a large platter, arrange pork, chicken, shrimp, cucumbers, and tomatoes on the lettuce leaves. Leave a space in the center of the platter for the hot dish described below:

3 tablespoons salad oil

2 chicken livers, cut into small pieces

⅔ cup minced onion

1 clove garlic, crushed

⅔ cup minced green pepper

⅔ cup chopped mushrooms

salt and pepper

m.s.g.

¼ pound vermicelli

Brown livers, onion, garlic, and green pepper in the hot oil. Add mushrooms, salt, pepper, and m.s.g. Stir-fry for 1–2 minutes. Boil vermicelli according to directions on the package. Drain. Mix well with the sauce. Add to the center of the salad platter.

Water Chestnut Salad

Yam Haew Chin

3 tablespoons salad oil
1 clove garlic, crushed
½ cup minced scallions
⅔ cup thinly sliced pork
6 raw shrimp, cleaned and
  cut into small pieces
4 tablespoons soy sauce
2 tablespoons sugar

2 tablespoons lemon juice
1¼ cups water chestnuts,
  thinly sliced
salt and pepper
m.s.g.
lettuce leaves
parsley sprigs

Brown garlic and scallions in the hot salad oil. Add pork and stir-fry until brown. Add shrimp and stir-fry until done. Stir in soy sauce, sugar, and lemon juice. Cook over low heat 2–3 minutes. Add water chestnuts and remaining seasonings. Stir-fry another minute. Serve immediately on lettuce leaves and garnish with sprigs of parsley.

Salad of Rose Petals

Yam Kulab

Roses are as lovely to eat as they are to look at. Try them this way.

2 *full-blown roses*
2 *tablespoons soy sauce*
2 *tablespoons lemon juice*
1 *teaspoon sugar*
1 *tablespoon chopped peanuts*
salt
m.s.g.
¼ *pound cooked pork, cut into small pieces*
6 *cooked shrimp, cut into small pieces*
lettuce leaves
1 *tablespoon salad oil*
1 *clove garlic, crushed*
½ *cup minced scallions*

Remove petals from the roses and cut them into small pieces. Combine soy sauce, lemon juice, sugar, peanuts, salt, and m.s.g. Add the rose petals, pork, and shrimp. Place the mixture on fresh lettuce leaves. Brown the garlic and minced scallions in a small frying pan. Pour hot on top of the salad and serve immediately.

❧ Meats ❧

Nüa

Pork Roast
Mu Op

4 pounds pork, rib, loin, or rolled shoulder

Combine and rub well into the meat:

2 *teaspoons cumin*
6 *small cloves of garlic, crushed*

$\frac{1}{2}$ *teaspoon pepper*
$\frac{1}{2}$ *teaspoon salt*

Place a pineapple rind (or several slices of canned pineapple) on top of the roast. Bake it in an oven preheated to 350 degrees, 40 minutes to the pound.

Combine:

4 *tablespoons soy sauce*
$\frac{1}{2}$ *cup vinegar*
6 *tablespoons brown sugar*
6 *tablespoons chopped parsley*
m.s.g.

When the roast is done, discard the pineapple rind. Baste the meat with 3 or 4 tablespoons of the soy sauce mixture. Return it to the oven for 10–15 minutes. Take it out again and baste it with more of the mixture. Do this three times. Remove roast to a platter. Pour remaining sauce into baking pan and heat it with the drippings. If the fat seems excessive, some of it may be removed first. Serve this as a gravy with the roast. Garnish the roast with fresh pineapple and parsley and serve with rice.

Sweet Pork

Mu Wan

Here is a kind of stew that is not only delicious but painless to prepare. It makes an excellent guest meal because it may be prepared in advance and reheated. It is served, of course, with rice.

2½ *pounds boned pork*
1 *clove garlic, crushed*
½ *cup brown sugar*
¼ *cup soy sauce*
1 *cup water*
1 *teaspoon cumin*
½ *teaspoon salt*
m.s.g.
chopped chives or chopped
 parsley

Combine all the ingredients except the meat and bring to a boil. Add the pork either in one piece or cut up. Cover and simmer over low heat for an hour or until meat is done. Remove cover and simmer for another hour or more or until liquid is reduced to less than half the original amount. Turn the meat over 2 or 3 times during cooking so that both sides become well coated with the liquid. The sauce should have a thick syrupy consistency when done. Serve cut into serving pieces garnished with chopped chives or parsley.

Barbecued Spareribs
Kaduk Mu

4 *pounds spareribs*
1 *clove garlic, crushed*
⅔ *cup soy sauce*
4 *tablespoons sugar*
1 *teaspoon salt*
½ *teaspoon pepper*
m.s.g.

Combine garlic, soy sauce, sugar, salt, pepper, and m.s.g. in a flat baking dish. Marinate spareribs 1–2 hours in the mixture, turning them over once or twice in that time. Ribs may then be barbecued over a charcoal fire and basted frequently with the sauce or they may be broiled. They may also be baked in a slow oven (325 degrees) for 2 hours in the baking dish in which they were marinated. They should be basted frequently.

Siamese Hamburgers
Luk Nüa

1 *pound chopped pork*
1 *pound chopped beef*
2 *cloves garlic, crushed*
2 *teaspoons ground coriander*
1 *teaspoon freshly ground*
  nutmeg

1 *teaspoon pepper*
½ *cup chopped scallions, both*
  green and white parts
2 *eggs, beaten*
salt
m.s.g.

Combine all the ingredients and form small balls. Brown in ¼ inch of hot cooking fat. Drain and serve. Serves 3–5.

Pork and Shrimp, Sweet and Sour with String Beans

Phat Priu Wan

Phat Priu Wan means a sweet and sour stir-fry. It is very often made with Chinese snow peas. Unhappily this delectable vegetable is not often available in our vegetable markets. I have found string beans a good substitute. Chinese cabbage or ordinary cabbage is almost as good, as is broccoli. Even sliced cucumbers and tomatoes may be used. The main thing is not to overcook the vegetable. Keep everything crisp and serve as soon as it is done.

3 *tablespoons salad oil*
4 *cloves garlic, crushed*
1 *pound boned pork, cut into small thin slices*
1 *pound raw shrimp, shelled and deveined*
3 *tablespoons soy sauce*
¼ *cup water*

2 *tablespoons sugar*
2 *tablespoons vinegar*
1 *teaspoon pepper*
1 *teaspoon salt*
m.s.g.
1 *package partially defrosted French-cut string beans*

Brown the garlic in the hot oil. Add the pork and stir-fry over high heat until the meat is well browned. Add the shrimp and stir-fry for a minute or two. Add the soy sauce, water, sugar, vinegar, pepper, salt, and m.s.g. Stir-fry for another minute, cover the pan, and cook over low heat for 10 minutes or until pork and shrimp are done. Add the string beans. Turn up heat and stir-fry until string beans are heated through. The beans should be crisp.

Sweet and Sour Pork

Mu Priu Wan

Using 2 pounds of pork cut into small pieces, follow the same procedure as in Sweet and Sour Chicken (page 76). Be sure the meat is well done before the rest of the ingredients are added.

Rama Bathing

Phra Ram Long Song

This was served to us at a Vietnamese home as a Vietnamese specialty. We learned later that there was a Laotian version which is almost identical, as well as a Thai version. Thin sesame seed crackers are my substitute for the rice wafers which usually go with this dish.

2 *pounds sirloin steak or*
   other tender beef
1½ *cups water*
1½ *cups vinegar*

1 *tablespoon sugar*
1 *bay leaf*
thin sesame seed crackers

GREENS (enough for 4–5 portions):
   lettuce leaves
   fresh mint or watercress
   chicory
   any other greens of your
     choice

½ cup peanuts, finely pounded
1 clove garlic, crushed
¼ teaspoon pepper
2 tablespoons sugar
¼ cup vinegar
dash of tabasco
salad oil

Cut the meat in thin slices on the bias. Arrange on a platter. Wash all the greens and arrange on another platter. Make the sauce. Add a little salad oil to give it a spreading consistency. Bring your electric skillet or hibachi to the table. Combine in it the water, vinegar, sugar, and bay leaf. Have the sliced beef, greens, sauce, and crackers at the table. Sit down. When the liquid boils, each person may pick up some meat with a fork or chopsticks and drop it into the skillet. In the meantime, take a lettuce leaf. Arrange smaller greens on it. Take your meat out (don't cook it too long) and place it on top of the greens. Spoon some sauce on top and roll it up. It's fun to do and delicious to eat. Rice may be served with this or later.

Rama Bathing

Phra Ram Long Song

(Thai Version)

1 *large coconut*
1½ *cups water*
1 *tablespoon soy sauce*
1 *tablespoon sugar*
1 *teaspoon curry paste for meat (page 35)*
½ *tablespoon salt*
m.s.g.
2 *pounds sirloin steak or other tender beef, cut in thin slices on the bias*
1 *teaspoon cornstarch, dissolved in a little water*
1 *cup finely chopped peanuts*
1 *package frozen whole leaf spinach, cooked according to directions*

Grate the coconut. Yield is approximately 3 cups. Combine coconut and water in a saucepan and bring to a boil. Let stand a few minutes until cool. Put pulp in a strainer. Press all the cream out and discard the pulp. Add the soy sauce, sugar, curry paste, salt, m.s.g., and beef. Cover and simmer 20 minutes. Add cornstarch and peanuts and cook 5 minutes longer or until thickened. Pour over spinach.

 Poultry

Kai Lae Pet

Roasted Duck

Pet Op

Our cook suddenly left us one day, and our not very shy wash girl pleaded for a chance to do her job. She turned out to be a better cook than the cook and this recipe was her first dinner. Served with duck sauce (page 95), it makes a sumptuous appearance at your table.

1 5-*pound duck*

Rub with garlic and season the inside with salt.

DRESSING:

3 *tablespoons butter*
giblets from the duck, cut
  into very small pieces
1 *medium onion, chopped*
1 *clove garlic, crushed*
¼ *teaspoon salt*
½ *teaspoon pepper*

2 *tablespoons soy sauce*
1 *cup uncooked rice*
1 *cup sliced mushrooms*
1¼ *cups pre-heated stock*
  (page 44)
m.s.g.

Melt butter in a frying pan and sauté the giblets. Add onion and garlic and stir-fry until onion is translucent. Add salt, pepper, and soy sauce and stir. Then add rice and stir-fry 2–3 minutes. Add mushrooms and stir-fry one more minute. Add stock and m.s.g. Cook over low heat a few minutes, stirring frequently until most of the liquid is absorbed. Allow to cool. Stuff the duck loosely and truss. Roast in a low oven (325 degrees) allowing 30 minutes to the pound. Baste every half hour.

Roasted Chicken
Kai Op

A roasting chicken may be cooked in the same way as the duck. Baste frequently with melted butter to keep it moist.

Chicken with Ginger
Kai Phat Khing

1 3½-pound chicken
¾ cup chopped scallions, both green and white parts
2 cloves garlic, crushed
3 tablespoons salad oil
¼ cup minced fresh or crystallized ginger
1½ tablespoons soy sauce
1½ tablespoons vinegar
1½ tablespoons sugar
¼ teaspoon salt
¼ teaspoon pepper
½ cup stock
1 cup mushrooms, sliced
parsley

Bone and cut the chicken into small pieces. Set aside. Sauté scallions and garlic in the oil. Add ginger, soy sauce, vinegar, and sugar. Stir until sugar dissolves. Add chicken and stir-fry 2–3 minutes. Add salt, pepper, and stock. Bring to a boil, then cover and simmer over low heat until chicken is done, about ½ hour. Add mushrooms and cook for 5 minutes longer. Garnish with parsley and serve with boiled rice.

Siamese Chicken in Coconut Cream
Kai Penang

No substitute will do for the coconut cream in this wonderful concoction. I prefer the Laotian version (page 75) with the chicken dressed. The Thai version omits the rice but has a sauce to be poured over the chicken.

1 3–4 *pound young chicken, rubbed with salt and garlic*
1 *large coconut to make 2 cups coconut cream*
½ *teaspoon pepper*
½ *teaspoon salt*
1 *teaspoon ground caraway seeds*
1 *teaspoon ground coriander seeds*

1 *tablespoon soy sauce*
1 *slice lemon*
2 *dried red chili peppers (remove seeds)*
2 *teaspoons sugar*
m.s.g.
1 *teaspoon anchovy paste*
¼ *cup finely chopped peanuts*
parsley sprigs

Grate the coconut. Combine it with 2 cups of water and bring the grated coconut to a boil. Let stand until cool. Strain the cream and discard the pulp. Put the chicken and the coconut cream in a large covered pot and simmer for an hour or until chicken is done. Remove chicken to a serving bowl and keep warm. Boil the cream until it is reduced to a cupful. Add the other ingredients, mix well, and simmer for 15 minutes. Remove the chilies. Pour the sauce over the chicken and garnish with sprigs of parsley.

Laotian Chicken in Coconut Cream

Kai Penang

1 3–4 *pound young chicken,*
  rubbed with salt and garlic
1 *large coconut to make* 2
  cups coconut cream
2 *teaspoons soy sauce*

DRESSING:

¼ *pound pork sausage*	½ *teaspoon pepper*
1 *medium onion, minced*	¼ *teaspoon cayenne pepper*
¼ *teaspoon cinnamon*	*m.s.g.*
2 *tablespoons dried mint*	⅓ *cup finely chopped peanuts*
leaves	½ *cup uncooked rice*
½ *teaspoon salt*	¾ *cup coconut cream*

Grate the coconut. Yield is approximately 3 cups. Pour ¾ cup boiling water over it. Let stand a few minutes, then put pulp through a strainer and use this coconut milk for the dressing. Add 1½ cups hot water to the same coconut pulp. Bring to a boil. Let stand until cool. Strain the cream and discard the pulp. Use this cream to cook the chicken. In a large frying pan, brown the sausage meat, breaking it into bits with a fork. Add onions and brown. Stir in cinnamon, mint, salt, pepper, and m.s.g. Add peanuts and rice and stir-fry for a minute or two. Then add first coconut cream yield and simmer over low heat, stirring frequently until most of the liquid is absorbed. Cool. Stuff the chicken and truss. Place it in a pot with the second coconut cream yield which has been seasoned with soy sauce. Cover the pot and cook over low heat for 1½ hours or until chicken is tender.

Sweet and Sour Chicken
Kai Priu Wan

1 3–4 *pound chicken*
1 *cucumber, peeled and sliced*
1 *medium-sized onion, sliced*
2 *medium-sized tomatoes, quartered*
2 *medium-sized green peppers, cut into squares*
½ *cup vinegar*
½ *cup sugar*
¼ *cup soy sauce*
½ *teaspoon salt*
dash of cayenne pepper
m.s.g.
1 *teaspoon cornstarch, dissolved in 2 tablespoons water*
2 *cloves garlic, crushed*
4 *tablespoons salad oil*

Bone the chicken and cut into small pieces. Cut up the vegetables. Set aside. Combine in a small bowl the vinegar, sugar, soy sauce, salt, cayenne, and m.s.g. Brown the garlic in hot oil. Stir-fry the chicken until well done. Add the vegetables and stir-fry for a minute or so. Add the sauce and stir, then cover and cook 2–3 minutes. Stir in the cornstarch paste and cook until the sauce thickens slightly. Do not overcook the vegetables.

Chicken with Cabbage

Kai Dom Kap Kalampi

1 3½-pound chicken, cut up
  into serving pieces
1 clove garlic, crushed
3 tablespoons salad oil
½ teaspoon ground coriander
½ teaspoon pepper
½ teaspoon salt
m.s.g.

1 teaspoon sugar
1 tablespoon soy sauce
1 cup stock (page 44)
3 cups thinly sliced-cabbage
1 cup sour cream (page 35
  coconut cream in place of
  sour cream)

Fry the garlic in hot oil. Brown the chicken lightly. Stir in the remaining ingredients except the cabbage and sour cream. Bring to a boil, then cover and simmer over low heat for an hour or until chicken is done. Add the cabbage. Mix well. Cover and cook 10 minutes longer. Do not overcook the cabbage. Stir in the sour cream and cook until heated through.

✿ Fish and Sea Foods ✿

Pla Lae Ahan Thale

Next to rice, fish is the most important food in the Thai diet. Just as the land is so richly productive of rice, the waters are equally productive of fish and other sea food.

Generally speaking, the Thai like their larger fish (which are served with the head on) either fried or steamed, served with ginger sauce or broiled over charcoal and served with *nam prik* (p. 86–87) or *lon* (p. 93). A smaller fish, *pla tu,* which resembles a herring, is usually steamed and then fried crisp and served with raw or cooked vegetables and the fish sauce, *nam pla.* This is considered a most ordinary meal. The *pla tu* may be bought already steamed from the market or even from the traveling vendor right at your front door. Then there are the dried and smoked fish—little things like minnows are delicious. Dry and salty, they are eaten with curries or with drinks. Shell fish are also plentiful. In Thailand prawns, shrimp, and crab are eaten as often as we eat hamburgers.

Sweet and Sour Fried Fish
with Ginger Sauce
Pla Priu Wan Khing

This dish is often made using a large reddish-skinned fish called *pla kapong daeng*. The sauce below is excellent and suitable for most of the fish available at our markets, either whole or filleted, and it may be used on poached, baked, or fried fish.

1 3-*pound fish, cleaned*	*parsley sprigs*

Rub the fish generously with oil, dredge in salted flour, and fry in ¼ inch of hot oil until golden brown on both sides. This will take from 3 to 5 minutes. Test with fork to see if it is done. Drain on absorbent paper. Serve with ginger sauce poured over it and garnish with parsley.

GINGER SAUCE :

3 *tablespoons minced fresh or crystallized ginger*	¼ *cup chopped mushrooms*
¼ *cup sugar*	¼ *cup chopped scallions, both green and white parts*
¼ *cup vinegar*	1 *teaspoon cornstarch, dissolved in 1 tablespoon water*
1 *tablespoon soy sauce*	
1 *cup water*	
salt and m.s.g.	

Combine ginger, sugar, vinegar, soy sauce, water, salt, and m.s.g. Simmer for 10 minutes. Add mushrooms and scallions and cook a few minutes longer or until mushrooms are tender. Stir in cornstarch paste and simmer a minute or so until sauce thickens. Serve immediately over fish.

Fried Shrimp Balls

Thotman Kung

2 cups cooked shrimp
1 clove garlic
½ teaspoon pepper
1 teaspoon ground coriander
½ teaspoon freshly grated
   nutmeg

¼ cup minced scallions,
   both green and white parts
1 egg beaten
¼ teaspoon salt
m.s.g.

Mash the shrimp with a fork or put through a food grinder. Add all the other ingredients and mix well. Form small balls and brown in ¼ inch of hot cooking fat for about 5 minutes. Drain on absorbent paper.

Crab and Broccoli

Phat Pak

1 clove garlic, crushed
2 tablespoons salad oil
½ teaspoon pepper
¼ teaspoon salt
m.s.g.
½ cup stock (page 44)
2 tablespoons soy sauce

1 cup cooked crab meat
1 box frozen broccoli, par-
   boiled
1 teaspoon cornstarch, dissolved in 1 tablespoon
   water

Fry garlic in the hot oil. Add salt, pepper, m.s.g., stock, and soy sauce. Bring to the boiling point. Add crab meat and broccoli and stir-fry carefully, trying not to shred the crab meat. Broccoli should remain crisp. Add cornstarch paste and cook a minute or two until sauce thickens.

Deviled Crab

Pu Cha

4 or 5 *medium-size boiled*
  crabs
$\frac{1}{4}$ *cup finely minced pork*
1 *clove garlic, crushed*

$\frac{1}{2}$ *teaspoon coriander*
$\frac{1}{4}$ *teaspoon pepper*
1 *egg, beaten*
1 *tablespoon chopped parsley*

Remove the crab meat and wash the shells well. To each cup of meat add the above seasoning and return to the shells and steam 5 minutes. A frying pan with a tight cover may be used. One-quarter inch of water is sufficient. Or they may be deep fried instead.

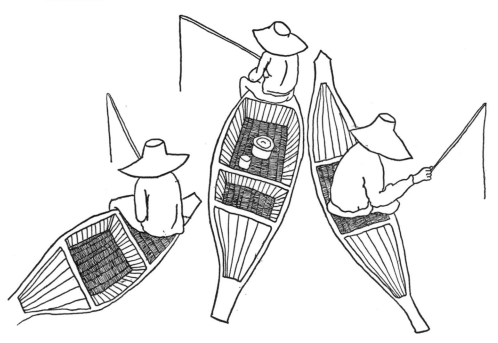

☙ Special Dishes ☙

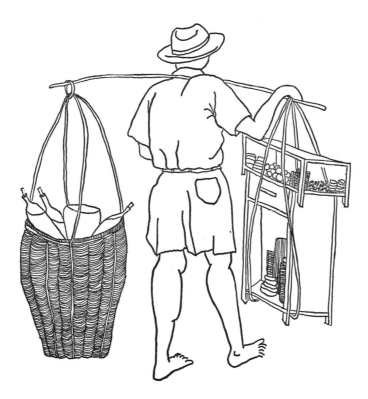

Some of the recipes in this chapter are drastically adapted to suit the Western menu and taste. Some do not fit into other categories of the book, but make excellent cocktail food. This may be a miscellaneous collection but should not be overlooked.

Nam Prik Canapés I

The most popular and commonly-eaten dish in Thailand after rice and fish is a sauce known as *nam prik*. It is used on rice and fish as well as on raw and cooked vegetables. It is so exotic and strange to the foreigner that few come to like it. Often it is the large quantity of chili peppers that scares the non-Thai away. There are many varieties of *nam prik,* and probably no two cooks ever use the same recipe. But it is the mark of a good cook to make a good one. I have substituted olives and green (unripened) pear for tamarind and green mango.

As a canapé, it is just the sort of food you would like with cocktails, salty and tangy. But if you want to be daring, try it on boiled vegetables, a bland baked or broiled fish, or on boiled rice.

3 *tablespoons smoked bone-less herring, finely minced*
2 *tablespoons minced stuffed green olives*
1 *clove garlic, crushed*
1½ *teaspoons anchovy paste*

1 *teaspoon brown sugar*
2 *tablespoons lemon juice*
½ *teaspoon soy sauce*
Tabasco sauce to taste
m.s.g.

Mince the fish and olives as finely as possible. Put the garlic through a press. Add the remaining ingredients and mix well. Place a slice of cucumber or tomato on crisp unsalted crackers, or cut small rounds of bread, and top with a mound of *nam prik*. Celery may also be stuffed with *nam prik*.

Yield about ½ cup, enough for canapés for 4–5.

Nam Prik Canapés 2

Substitute ¼ cup coarsely grated hard green pear for the olives in the above recipe.

Nam Prik Canapés 3

2 *tablespoons anchovy fillets, finely minced*
1 *clove garlic, crushed*
1 *cup coarsely grated hard green (unripened) pear*
2 *tablespoons anchovy paste*

2 *teaspoons brown sugar*
3 *tablespoons lemon juice*
½ *teaspoon soy sauce*
Tabasco sauce to taste
m.s.g.

Follow the same procedure as in Nam Prik 1.

Curry Puffs

Here is a delicious hot appetizer which may be prepared in advance and kept in the refrigerator to be baked when guests arrive. Your favorite pie crust dough may be used instead of the one offered here.

1 *package (3 ounces) cream*   ¼ *pound butter*
   cheese   1 *cup sifted flour*

Combine these three ingredients first with a fork and then work quickly with the hands. Divide dough in half and chill.

FILLING:
   2 *tablespoons butter*
   ½ *pound ground beef*
   ¼ *cup minced onion*
   1 *clove garlic, crushed*
   2 *teaspoons curry paste for*
      meat (page 35)
   ½ *cup water*
   ½ *teaspoon salt*
   m.s.g.

Melt butter in a frying pan. Add the meat, onions, and garlic. Stir-fry over high heat until brown. Stir in the remaining ingredients and simmer covered for ½ hour. Cool. Roll dough out to ⅛-inch thickness between two pieces of waxed paper. Cut with round cutter or water tumbler. Place small amount of filling on each round of dough. Fold in half, pressing edges together with fingers to seal, making a half-circle. Bake on ungreased cookie sheet in a moderate oven (350 degrees) until golden, about 20 minutes. Makes about 1½ dozen puffs.

Shrimp Rolls

Hae Kung

Prepare the curry puff dough (p. 88), or if a less rich dough is preferred, your own pie crust dough may be used. These shrimp rolls may be served with sweet and sour sauce or eaten as is.

FILLING:

2 *tablespoons melted butter*	½ *teaspoon ground coriander*
1 *clove garlic*	¼ *teaspoon pepper*
½ *pound uncooked shrimp,*	¼ *teaspoon salt*
shelled, deveined and minced	1 *tablespoon soy sauce*

Melt butter in a frying pan. Add garlic and shrimp and stir-fry until shrimp turn pink. Add remaining ingredients and cook two or three minutes. Roll out the dough to ⅛-inch thickness and cut with a round cutter about 3–4 inches in diameter. Place a tablespoon of the filling on each round, fold one side of dough over the other, and press together making a sausage-like form. Bake in a moderate oven (350 degrees) for 20 minutes or until golden. Serve hot. Makes about one dozen rolls.

SWEET AND SOUR SAUCE:

2 *tablespoons minced mush-*	¼ *cup vinegar*
rooms	2 *tablespoon soy sauce*
1 *teaspoon minced fresh or*	¼ *cup water*
crystallized ginger	¼ *teaspoon salt*
2 *tablespoons minced scal-*	*m.s.g.*
lions	½ *teaspoon cornstarch dissolved*
¼ *cup sugar*	*in 2 tablespoons water*

Combine in a saucepan all the ingredients except cornstarch. Bring to a boil and simmer 10 minutes. Add cornstarch paste and cook until thickened.

Pork and Crab Rolls
Pratat Lom

Prepare the curry puff dough (p. 88) or your own pie crust dough.

FILLING:

2 *tablespoons melted butter*	¼ *teaspoon pepper*
½ *cup minced pork*	¼ *teaspoon salt*
½ *cup minced cooked crabmeat*	1 *tablespoon soy sauce*
½ *teaspoon ground coriander*	

Melt butter in a frying pan. Add garlic and pork and stir-fry until done. Add remaining ingredients and cook two or three minutes. Roll out the dough to ⅛-inch thickness and cut into 3-inch squares. Place one tablespoon of filling on each square and bring the corners of the square to meet in the center. Pinch the edges together to seal. Bake in a moderate oven (350 degrees) for 20 minutes or until golden. Yields about 1 dozen rolls. Serve hot with the following sauce:

2 *tablespoon soy sauce mixed with* 1 *tablespoon vinegar*

Plump Horses
Ma Uan

This is a delicious meat custard which does well in place of soup.

4 *eggs*
¼ *cup minced uncooked pork*
¼ *cup minced uncooked chicken*
2 *tablespoons minced scallions*
1½ *cups chicken stock*

1 *teaspoon ground coriander*
½ *teaspoon pepper*
½ *teaspoon salt*
1 *teaspoon sugar*
1 *clove garlic, crushed*
m.s.g.
chopped parsley

Beat the eggs. Stir in everything else. Pour into individual custard cups. Set the cups in a pan, preferably on a rack, and pour simmering water around them halfway up the cups. Cover the pan and cook over a low flame until a silver knife comes out clean. This takes from 20–30 minutes. The water should be barely simmering during the cooking. These are best served hot in the cups, garnished with chopped parsley, or you may cool and invert the cups. Serves 4.

Omelet Stuffed with Pork

Rum

2 *tablespoons salad oil*
1 *clove garlic, crushed*
½ *cup minced uncooked pork*
2 *tablespoons soy sauce*
salt and pepper

m.s.g.
parsley sprigs
2 *eggs, well beaten*
1 *tablespoon butter*

Brown garlic in hot oil. Add pork and stir-fry until done. Add soy sauce, salt, pepper, and m.s.g. Cook for 5 minutes and set aside. Melt butter in a small skillet. Pour just enough egg to make a thin omelet about 5 inches in diameter. Turn when done as you would a pancake and cook on the other side. Place the omelet on a warm plate. Put a large sprig of parsley in the center of the omelet, then 2 tablespoons of the meat mixture. Fold one side over, then the other, and then the ends, to make a square bundle. Keep warm while you make more. Garnish with a slice of red chili pepper or pimento.

Omelet Stuffed with Shrimp

La Tieng

Instead of pork use chopped shrimp or half pork and half shrimp. Add 1 teaspoon ground coriander seed to the stuffing.

Boiled Sauce
Lon

This boiled sauce is served hot as a salad dressing on greens, shrimp, or crab meat salad. It may also be served on cooked vegetables such as cauliflower, asparagus, broccoli, or string beans. If a plainer dressing is preferred, it may be made by leaving out the shellfish. The Thai make *lon* in many different ways using makrut (Kaffir lime) juice, tamarind pulp, coconut cream, and salted fish.

Crab Sauce
Pu Lon

2 *eggs, beaten*
¼ *cup sweet cream*
¼ *cup cooked crab meat, shredded*
1 *teaspoon dry hot mustard*
1 *tablespoon salad oil*
1 *tablespoon lemon juice*

¼ *teaspoon pepper*
¼ *teaspoon salt*
½ *teaspoon sugar*
⅛ *teaspoon Tabasco sauce (optional)*
m.s.g.

Combine ingredients in the top half of a double boiler and cook over hot water, stirring constantly until thick. Serve immediately.

Shrimp Sauce
Kung Lon

Substitute cooked shrimp for the crab meat.

Peach Chutney

Chutney made from mangoes is an Indian idea. The Thai grow plenty of mangoes but they don't cook them this way. I have always believed chutney to be an essential complement to a curry, and in Bankgok most foreigners felt the same way. Jars of imported chutney were always available in the market at an incredibly high price. Peaches and pears make a very good substitute for mangoes. You don't really have to go to the bother of the canning process. Half the recipe will keep for a long time in your refrigerator in an unsealed but sterilized jar.

8 *cups firm peaches, peeled and chopped*
1 *lemon, seeded and chopped*
2 *cloves garlic, crushed*
1½ *cups seedless raisins*
½ *cup fresh or crystallized ginger, minced*

2 *teaspoons salt*
1 *teaspoon cayenne pepper*
2½ *cups cider vinegar*
3½ *cups brown sugar*
¾ *cup green pepper, chopped*

Combine ingredients and cook over low heat for 3 hours. Seal in sterilized jars. Yield is about 2 ½ quarts.

Pear Chutney

Pears may be used instead of peaches or both may be used together. In combination I like the proportion of 6 cups of peaches to 2 cups of pears.

Duck Sauce

This chutney is most often served with duck and chicken. It is of Chinese origin but very much enjoyed by the Thai. It should have a sweet-sour taste. The amount of sugar used is dependent on the tartness of the fruit. Taste it after it cooks a while and add more sugar if needed. Be sure the fruit you use is well ripened.

3 *cups fresh ripe plums
(skins and pits removed)*
2½ *cups fresh ripe or dried
apricots (pits removed)*
1½ *cups fresh or canned
pineapple (strawberries,
peaches, or pears may be
substituted)*
¾ *cup vinegar*
1½–3½ *cups sugar*

Cut fruit in very small pieces. Measure and combine in a large pot. Add vinegar and sugar. Stir and bring to the boiling point. Then simmer 1½–2 hours over low heat or until it thickens. Seal in sterilized jars and store in a cool place. Yield is about 2 quarts.

 Desserts

Khong Wan

Lotus seeds, mung beans, rice flour, glutinous rice, palm sugar, cassava roots, and coconut are some of the common ingredients for Thai desserts. The Thai like their desserts to have a fragrance, so they soak jasmine and other aromatic flowers in water and then use this scented water to make a syrup. Bland seeds or beans are cooked in the syrup to make what is known as a liquid sweet. An aromatic candle is often burned next to cakes or cookies in a closed container to impart a scent to them, or the dessert is placed next to fragrant flowers overnight. Cookies are sometimes garnished with a bit of gold leaf.

The recipes I have included in this section adapt well to substitution and are familiar to Western taste.

Golden Cookies
Tong Ek

The Thai use melon or lotus seeds or any of the nuts, especially peanuts. Although this recipe is a far cry from the real thing, it is rich and tasty.

1 *cup packaged shredded coconut*	¾ *cup sugar*
	½ *cup butter*
½ *cup milk*	2 *egg yolks*
1½ *cups flour*	¾ *cup finely chopped pecans*
1 *teaspoon baking powder*	*whole pecans*

Combine milk and coconut and bring to a boil. Let cool and then press through a strainer until the pulp is dry. Discard the pulp and set the coconut cream aside. Sift the dry ingredients and mix well. Cut in the butter until the dough looks like coarse meal. Add the egg yolks, nuts, and coconut cream and mix thoroughly. Drop from a teaspoon on a greased and floured cookie sheet. Press flat with the back of a spoon. Top with a pecan nut. Bake in a 350-degree oven 15–20 minutes or until golden brown. Yields approximately 2½ dozen.

Siamese Pancakes
Khanom Klok

2 *cups packaged shredded coconut*	½ *cup flour*
1½ *cups milk*	4 *tablespoons sugar*
4 *eggs, beaten*	*dash salt*

Combine milk and coconut in a saucepan. Bring to a boil. Let stand a half hour or so. Press the milk from the coconut using a strainer and discard the pulp. Stir the beaten eggs into the milk. Then sift and add the dry ingredients. Stir until it is the consistency of cream. Grease a hot skillet. Drop the batter by the spoonful onto the skillet. When brown, turn and brown the other side. Serve for dessert sprinkled with confectioner's sugar.

Pumpkin Custard
Sangkhaya

Here is an unusual dessert that appeals to everyone. The trick is not to break the pumpkin when removing it from the steamer. The Thai use palm sugar to sweeten the custard, but I have never found it in this country. They also make *sangkhaya* using a very young coconut instead of pumpkin but, like palm sugar, young coconuts are hard to come by.

1 *pumpkin about 9 inches in diameter*
1 *cup packaged shredded coconut*
1 *cup milk*
½ *cup cream, scalded*
3 *eggs, beaten*
½ *cup brown sugar*
⅛ *teaspoon salt*

Cut a hole in the top of the pumpkin to remove the stem. Scoop out the seeds and pulp. Wash and drain well. Combine coconut and milk in a pan, bring to a boil, then cool. Press all the milk from the coconut using a strainer and discard the pulp. Combine this coconut milk with the cream, beaten eggs, brown sugar, and salt and beat until well blended. Pour the custard into the pumpkin and place on a rack in a steamer over very low heat until the custard is done. Test by inserting a silver knife into the custard. An ordinary cooking pot with a tight cover may be used. About ½ inch of water is usually enough. Remove the pumpkin carefully to a shallow bowl and chill it. Slice it at the table as you would a pie.

Three Chums

Khanom Sam Klü

When these sesame seed fritters are to be served at weddings, they are made in groups of three and, as they fry, they predict the couple's future. If the three balls stick together, the marriage will succeed and a child will be born. If one of the fritters breaks away, the couple will be childless. If all three fritters separate from each other, the marriage will go on the rocks. A very thick batter will surely keep the three together, as will a couple of toothpicks.

1 *cup packaged shredded coconut*
½ *cup brown sugar*
½ *cup milk*

½ *cup flour*
1 *teaspoon baking powder*
½ *cup sesame seeds*

BATTER:
1 *egg beaten*
⅓ *cup flour*
¼ *cup milk*
⅛ *teaspoon salt*
fat for frying

Combine coconut, sugar, and milk in a saucepan. Cook over a low flame, stirring frequently until thick and syrupy, about 10 minutes. Sift the flour and baking powder together. Mix in the sesame seeds. Add to the coconut mixture and mix thoroughly. Form small balls about an inch in diameter. Make a batter of the egg, flour, milk, and salt. Coat the balls well and fry in hot fat (375 degrees) until golden. Sprinkle with powdered sugar and serve warm. Yields 12–18 fritters.

Saffron Puffs

Khanom Sai Kai

This is a most wonderful confection. If you've never cared for doughnuts or crullers, you will change your mind when you try these.

½ teaspoon saffron
1 tablespoon boiling water
1 cup shredded coconut
½ cup milk
2 cups sifted flour
1 teaspoon baking powder

1 teaspoon soda
¾ cup buttermilk
¼ cup salad oil
1 egg beaten
fat for frying

Soak saffron in the boiling water. Combine milk and coconut in a saucepan. Bring to a boil, then cool. Put coconut in a strainer and press out the milk. Discard the pulp. Yield is less than ½ cup coconut cream. Sift dry ingredients together. Stir in buttermilk, oil, egg, dissolved saffron, and coconut cream. Drop with teaspoon (large amount will not cook through) into hot fat (375 degrees). Fry until golden. Drain on absorbent paper. The warm puffs are then rolled in a syrup which is made by boiling 2 cups granulated sugar and 1 cup water until thick. They are equally good rolled in pancake syrup, granulated or confectioners' sugar, or sprinkled with coconut. Yields 20–30 puffs.

Banana Puffs

Add one mashed ripe banana to batter and proceed as above.

Tapioca Pudding

Saku

2 *cups milk*	4 *tablespoons sugar*
2 *cups packaged shredded coconut*	3 *tablespoons quick-cooking tapioca*
2 *eggs*	¼ *teaspoon salt*

Combine milk and coconut in a saucepan. Bring to a boil then let stand a half hour. Press the milk from the coconut using a strainer and discard the pulp. Beat the egg whites until foamy. Add 2 tablespoons sugar and beat until soft peaks form. Let stand. Beat the yolks slightly. Add remaining sugar, coconut cream, tapioca, and salt. Cook over low heat, stirring constantly until the mixture boils. Keep stirring until the tapioca is well dissolved. Pour the hot mixture very slowly into the beaten egg whites, stirring constantly. Serve hot or cold with whipped cream or coconut cream, which may be made using 1 cup of milk pressed through 3 cups of shredded coconut. Use same procedure as above, then chill the cream.

Stewed Bananas

Kluai Chüam

4 *medium, firm bananas*	1 *cup water*
½ *cup sugar*	

Slice bananas in half lengthwise, then in half crosswise. Bring sugar and water to a boil. Add bananas and simmer uncovered 5–10 minutes or until bananas are transparent but not too soft. Serve hot topped with shredded coconut.

Fried Bananas and Coconut
Kluai Thot

Bananas are seen everywhere in Thailand. Several varieties grow abundantly throughout the year. Here are some of the many ways they are prepared.

4 *firm bananas*	2 *tablespoons sugar*
½ *cup packaged shredded*	1 *egg, beaten*
coconut	2 *tablespoons butter*
1½ *tablespoons flour*	

Peel bananas, cut in half lengthwise, then in half crosswise. Combine flour, sugar, and egg and coat the bananas generously. Then sauté for 5 minutes on both sides in melted butter. Serve hot.

Banana Chips
Kluai Chap

3 *firm bananas*	*oil or other fat for frying*
½ *cup lime juice*	*sugar*

Peel and slice the bananas very thin. Marinate them in lime juice 10–15 minutes. Fry in hot deep fat (375 degrees) until they are crisp and brown. Drain them on absorbent paper. Roll in granulated or confectioner's sugar.

Index